EXCUSE ME YOU MIND IF I WRITE YOU A POEM?

Adrian D. Weaver

Book Title Copyright © 2020 by Adrian D. Weaver. All Rights Reserved.

All rights reserved. No part of this book may be reproduced in any form or by any electronic or mechanical means including information storage and retrieval systems, without permission in writing from the author. The only exception is by a reviewer, who may quote short excerpts in a review.

Cover designed by Tammie T. Polk

This book is a work of fiction. Names, characters, places, and incidents either are products of the author's imagination or are used fictitiously. Any resemblance to actual persons, living or dead, events, or locales is entirely coincidental.

Adrian D. Weaver
Visit my website at www.AuthorName.com

Printed in the United States of America

First Printing: Aug 2017
Name of Company

ISBN-13 978-1-7354394-3-3

CONTENTS

Acknowledgements 6
Volume I 7
Special 8
Oceans, Beaches, and the Sun 11
July Kiss 13
Snow Queen 15
Whispers of My Heart 17
Letting Go of My Love 19
I Wasn't Finished Yet 21
Volume II 24
Stormy Eyes 25
Words from a Real Man 27
Seeking for a Star 28
Woman 30
You Are My White Rose 32
Lips of Rose Petals 34
I Give My Sword for Just a Hug 36
Hear Me Oh Queen 39
My Sleeping Beauty 41
She Wore Satin 43
The Show Begins at Three 45
Chocolate Rose 47
Mr. Wrong on Your Arm 49
Lady I Knew 52
The Painting at the Gallery 54
You Got Me 57
She Took Me 58
Redemption Is Now My Fame 61
Those Sexy Eyes of Yours 63
Undying Love 65

I Fell for You Lady	67
I've Never Had	68
My Girl Next Door	70
88 Keys of Seduction	71
To the Letter	76

Thanks....
To God, I would like to thank You for giving me my gift. You've giving me something so special. So hopefully, I can make many people see happiness, by these words. I write because You gave me, vision!

ACKNOWLEDGEMENTS

An 8th grade assignment to create a book of poetry, would turn into years of poems and creative writings. A teacher by the name of Rosa J. Barber, who just happen to be my grandmother, would help with the structure of writing poetry. I got an "A" on my assignment but never stopped writing. I was amazed that I could bring my visions into fruition. Rosa was able to harness this gift so I could show the world my emotions and creativeness on paper. The gift was able to grow into a manifestation of love and inspiration. For that, I thank her and dedicated this book to Ms. Rosa J. Barber.

In Loving Memory
Of
Jacqueline J. Weaver (Mom)

VOLUME I

SPECIAL

The first time I glanced
Into your eyes
Beauty they behold,
Yearning that lies

A scent of radiance
Smells of bliss
A smell so enchanting
It shall not be missed

Skin so soft,
As satin does shine
As chocolate as candy
So delicate and fine

Your lips are as petals
Resembling a rose
Deep with passion,
Passion explodes

A walk of integrity,
Sensuous and smooth
With grace and form,
As a butterfly move

Your utmost beauty
Of your body alone
Is as rare as a goddess
Of a siren's song

Your mind is as precious
As a diamond stone
The value of it
Could never be shown

All I've told,
Could not match you worth
Except for your mother,
Who gave you birth

You're the flame on my candle,
The star in my life
The rose on my stem,
The strength of my might

To you forever,
And yes loyal
No other person
Could be so special!

OCEANS, BEACHES, AND THE SUN

A salty gust, from the ocean spray
Nightfall began, a fallen day

The words of the waves, are calmly said
As it rushes to the beach, which lies ahead

The beach is so level, not a inch disturbed
This aging of nature, is truly superb

I took a young lady, to this lonely beach
The setting of the sun, seem to be at reach

Clinching her hand, we walked the waves
Sand all around, our path was made

I set on the beach, and so did she
My legs around, so close you see

She laid on my chest, a breath from my heart
I held her tightly never to be apart

I'll hold her forever, till all has ceased
But love her less, not the least

So I took her finger, and sketched I Love U
Whispered in her ear, I'll always have U

The moon has risen, not a cloud in the sky
So full for the earth, sensations so high

We slept on the beach, wrapped in our arms
The moon is our witness, fearing no harm

I love U my dear, I must say again
Woman, your my lover my friend

Trading in the ocean, the beach, including the sun
Without you my dear, these things are no fun

Now the day has close, and been put to rest
For the love I have, thank God I'm blessed

JULY KISS

A hot summer night, flowers at bloom,
I'm going to see one, for sure—soon

I step to darkness, soon to be light
A path of not knowing, blindness my sight

A fiery sky, from rocket below
Shadows of trees, begin to glow

I'm with this young lady, so beautiful to me
Grace and excellence, it doesn't take to see

We step together, as I prepared to leave
Me not knowing, this gift I receive

A virgin to her, lips and touch
Would an embrace to her, be to much

I said my good-byes, and stepped away

My heart said stop, this is the day

I looked back, into her eyes
This is the day, that would change our lives

Touching upon, her delicate lips
I kissed her, as if it was my last sip

God thank you, for this day in July
Thanks for answering my gracious reply

For you alone, knew my needs
You bless me with, your rarest seed

SNOW QUEEN

Silent to the cars, but loud to the eyes
Motionless playground, with gray covered skies

Snow so soft, as far as you can see
Sparkle of diamonds, is what it seems to be

A white picket fence, with swings and slides
The mighty oak tree, protects and hides

Suddenly a sound, disturbing the still
The presence of two, coming from the hill

Standing in the playground, as they left their trail
Leaving another behind, from her fascinating smell

Reliving the memories, of a schoolboy and girl
Far Far away, into this snow frost world

They slid down the slide and rode on the swings

Ran from each other, and made angels with wings

Time had passed, as the light grow dim
Glowing sparkles, accompany them

They walked to the fence, placing her on top
So much attention, she's loving it a lot

Close your eyes, so you may receive
This snowy gift, that I have retrieve

She closed them shut, as he reached to the ground
Silence arose, only windy sounds

To quiet for the eyes, with a need to know
What did she see, a crown made of snow

Her eyes lit up, from this wonderous sight
He placed it on her head, shining so bright

Gazing in her eyes, he kissed—her hand
Snugging her hands, this is what he said

Hundreds of queens, throughout have been seen
But you my lady, are the first snow queen!

WHISPERS OF MY HEART

The day I fell in love, the ocean roared
The day I fell in love, the skies opened poured
The day I fell in love, I fell in love with U
The day I fell in love, was the day I needed U

How many times, have I looked in your face
How many times, have I watched your grace
How many times, have I put you to sleep
How many times, have I calmed your weep

So many words, I'd like to say
So many words, not enough in a day
So many words, made like art
So many words, are treasured in my heart

These things I write, I write for you
For no other woman, measure to you

Your grace, your beauty, are treasure of the eyes
The most things I treasure, are the things inside

I've kissed your cheeks, left and right
I'll kiss your cheeks, every night
In dreams, In life, In present, In time
I'll love you always, til the sun is declined

LETTING GO OF MY LOVE

How much passion can one man withhold?
From the love of his life, that is in his soul

So, I write these things, I'm writing for you
Because this passion in me, I cannot withhold from you

The way you talk, and say your words
As joyful as the morning, as singing baby birds

You walk in a room, and outshine the lights
You walked in my life; the darkness seems bright

What would I've have done; without the love you gave?
I would have been a hopeless case, a timeless slave

Countless nights, the love we've made
Became one? We're more, I'm even been your shade.
And moments like these, were not meant to fade

Our hugs are different, it's a puzzle we pieced
Once we connect, our love was unleashed

Being in your presence, the giving of your time
I was just happy to be there, as you shine, shine, shine

I've finished these words, but not my love
You were given to me, from him above

I LOVE U!

I WASN'T FINISHED YET

Many days have past, many nights are gone
Some nights I'd died, when all went wrong

You're still the right hand of my heart,
The backbone of my spirit
Never seeing you again I sincerely fear it

My friends think I'm fine, but I can act a role
If they could see the torment, of my restless soul

The damn has broken, and flooded is on the ways
I look to the Lord, and deeply pray

A lonely man—I have but one regret
Oh Lord, I wasn't finished yet

My Image of her, is beautiful indeed
The warmth of her hugs, a vastly need

No man is complete, with no rib to provide
One life to live, but a thousand I've died

The moon and the sun are balances of the earth
Each step I take, I stumble I hurt

So should I accept, and go head and fall
Or tangle with advisor, and go for it all

A lonely man—I have but one regret
Oh Lord I wasn't finished yet

Our common ground, is our link to love
For our common ground is what we're made of

So here we are the Sun, and the star
Yet so close, but it seems so far

No matter where you go, what end of the earth
The love that we share, has a constant thirst

The water is there, the desert all around
The sand is plenty, from water I'll drown

This love I have, is only for U
I have but one regret
Oh Lord, My God—I just wasn't finished yet

VOLUME II

STORMY EYES

I've looked at the sky, in the dark night
Sky of diamonds, that shine so bright

I stood one night, not a care in the world
Gazing at a start, with the beauty of a pearl

A graceful passing, and then it was gone
Such a pretty star, not a trace was shown

So I vowed to see, to come again
She passed me over once more, my hand I extend

So, I grasp her hand, and held it tight
Letting her know, no harm this night

I sat her down, and look in her eyes
This was something more precious, than diamond lit skies

For the beauty in her eyes, was beauty alone
As if a star was trapped, in a rare gemstone

No stars, No moon, No planets around
Could compare to these precious eyes I've found

You are a treasure, more than you'll know
This I will treasure, in my heart – also

I may not see, this star again
But I'll never forget, my friend

WORDS FROM A REAL MAN

For the times, you've made me feel like a king
For the times, you've been the only one in my dream

For the times, I've looked deep into your eyes
For the times, I've witness that pretty smile

For the times, I've touched your silky skin
For the times, you've been just my friend

For this I give U, my undying hand
                From what you call
                  A Real Man!

SEEKING FOR A STAR

The moment I saw you, time was no more
This was one day, I could not ignore

A shooting star, had passed by my face
Only beauty and eloquence, was part of it space

As you shot by, you glance—into my eyes
For that short time in life, I was hypnotized

Hypnotize by what
Was it the star, the beauty, the eloquence, the smile?
Or was it that wanting desire, passion to be wild

Was it your eyes, your skin, your legs, your feet?
Or was it—I wanted, to keep you all for me?

Nevertheless, the beauty is seen
But inside the star, is a beautiful dream

No darkness in the world, could keep me from U
If I strive, it's you I pursue

I hear your words, and feel what you say
And hope to God, you think of me each longing day

Is there much more—to what I see?
If so enlighten me?

Now you are the one, that I seek
Now open your door and kiss me my sweet.

WOMAN

Woman, Woman, Woman
How many times must I call your name?
To let you know, I have a burning flame

A flame that burns, just for you
A flame that warms, my heart too

Do I grab your hand, and pull you near?
Do I kiss your face, from ear to ear?

Is it roses you want, Is it love you need?
My heart is open, fulfil that deed

Looking for warmth, I'll hold you tight
And let you know, you're in my life

To be held through the night, by someone who cares
This feeling I give, this feeling I share

So, when you close your eyes, think of me
Cause when I close mine, it's you I'll see

YOU ARE MY WHITE ROSE

Many nights have pass, since we've met
Since that time, I have no regrets

You change like the skies, you have reason too
No matter how you change, I'll never leaving you

And if a tear, should begin to fall
I'll be the net, to catch them all

I've seen you down, and seen your gloom
But you are that white rose, that glisten the room

The white rose itself, the most precious of them all
It's rarity and worth, are seen over all

If the stem of the rose, should bend from stress
I shall use my back, and give it some rest

And to keep that rose, from withering away
I'll crest you and hold you, through each trying day

Holding your hand, and having you near
I would feel so honored, Yes, I'm sincere

I've got your back, I'll support your goals
I'll be the man, to comfort your soul

Most of all my boo, you are my friend
To part with that, would mean my end

So, my friend, these are my words
The truth of my mouth, I've hope you heard

So, remember this rose, when placed in your eyes
You'll see what I see, in my heart that lies

              Until We Meet Again!

LIPS OF ROSE PETALS

When I see your lips, it's a glowing shine
Whether natural or colored, they're truly divine

A design of perfection, no flaw has been seen
As the great wonders of the world, captive as a stream

Each line, each curve carefully placed
Lips full, I drool, nothing went to waste

Lips are as pretty, as a tulip in bloom
Like a diamond in cased, that lights up the room

Even when you speak, they mesmerize me
You see, to me, a gem they will be

Each time I glance, as if the first
That beautiful design, god giveth at birth

If you could use my eye, and see what I see

You would be amazed, of what they do to me

A kiss on the jaw, of wine-colored lips
A print of temptations, I rather take a sip

These lips of temptation, are sweet Indeed
God's gift, God's blessing, truly out done deed

I GIVE MY SWORD FOR JUST A HUG

A Knight I am, courageous and brave
Trustworthy a gentleman, a man's been made

Honor thy sword, it shields my life
From battles of Wars, I pray each night

My sword is my heart, where it goes, I lie
To cleave it by the King, disgrace me—I'd die

I ride off to battle, with God in my heart
To fight for my kingdom, I must do my part

The outcry of swords, crashing together
Has taken its toll, is dying better

My arms weary, by the weight of the sword
Silence and peace, I ask you O Lord

No shield of War, can hide the pain
So, where do I go to shield this rain

There is but one, that can hold me tight
Rub my wounds, and guard my life

Am I less than a man, to feel so safe?
In your arms, I shall not forsake

My face has trails, covered with tears
O Lord My God, she's holding me near

I come from your bosom, with a silent moan
I look in your eyes, I just want to go home

My sword is my weapon, my sword is my life
But I'd give it up, for this one night

No screams No pain, just someone to hold
Someone who cares, the healing of my soul

I'd give my sword for just a hug
Did you hear me? I said
I'd give my sword for just a hug
If God grants me this wish from above

Here's Thy Sword
Amen!

HEAR ME OH QUEEN

There's the queen, in royal robes
Not gold but persona, shines to the globes

Beauty for her, a small choice of words
Rare and precious, is all I've heard

But would a jewel like her, listen to a rock
I've wiped my dust; I hope she's not shocked

Hear me Oh Queen
I am heard—but not always seen
I'm a peasant, but you are my dream
Hear me Oh Queen

I close my eyes, and wish I was near
She's royal blood, this I fear

A peasant I am, but a man I stand
Does it matter, should I descend my hand

The queen she is, thy throne she sits
I must voice my heart, and rely on my wit

Hear me Oh Queen
I am heard —but not always seen
I'm a peasant, but you are my dream
Hear me Oh Queen

Forgive me Oh Queen, I have something to say
That's been weighing my heart since your first day

There's no sight I've seen, more precious than U
Not ransom of jewels, not even morning dew

I've no materials, just the things from above
A sack of faith, a stack of hope, and abundance of love

So, hear me Oh Queen
I am heard – but not always seen
I'm a peasant, but you are my dream
So hear me Oh Queen, Do you see me Oh Queen

MY SLEEPING BEAUTY

Have you seen a night? With tears in the sky
Clouds all around, and not a spot dry

Lighting has struck, thunder has roared
Your lights are out, your thoughts—with the Lord

A candle I lit, such a dim glare
The house is still, calmness in the air

Woman—I lead, to the couch for rest
I pull you near, with your head to my chest

You fall asleep, with peace as your shield
You have no Idea, how this makes me feel

Your hair I stroke, I notice each strand
This one raining night, I'm your biggest fan
The flame of the candle, blending with your skin
You're already beautiful, you're golden my friend

The beat of your heart, tingles my spine
I'm one lucky man, to be part of your time

My beauty—asleep, resting away
There is no way in hell, I would trade this day

So, I kiss your cheeks, a grin I see
There's no mistaken, this is where I want to be

So now I sleep, with you in my arms
My sleeping beauty, my lovely charm

                Goodnight
                Woman

SHE WORE SATIN

Moment to treasure, I dance with U
Time to time, that thought I pursue

That night was special, woven in space
A lady in black, the look on my face

The lights were out, the candles were spies
They witness that lady, in a satin prize

T. Braxton was singing, with her band on stage
The living room cozy, our fingers engage

The music seductive, trembling our skin
Lost in your eyes, desire within

I plucked a rose, standing like a scholar
Place it on your lips, your heart would holler

The rose was red, deeper than the ocean

Against that black, I followed your motion

Your curves, you design, are from an expertise
That was carefully placed, remarkable to say the least

Loosely—I guided, letting it all fall
The rose was on a journey, an occasional stall

Trembles from the rose, dragging its petals
As you twitch from sensation, your body want settle

I embrace your torso, and hold it tight
As I dip your body, beauty's my sight

I peck your lips, and rub your cheeks
Kiss you gently, it's you I seek

Moments like these, will always last
But that black dress and curves will
Never pass

THE SHOW BEGINS AT THREE

You have on a pair of heels
That's the real deal
Such sex appeal
You have the right of way, I shall yield.

It something about the way you walk
That makes those heels talk
Hips sway like a hawk
Don't stop, I want you to walk

I love the way you stand, command
Demand from a man
His attention span
Forget Tyra Banks, I'm your biggest fan

Woman what's that
It's called and ankle strap
I feel like I been slapped
Woke up out my nap
Can I go where you're going, would that be a thought, perhaps

Stockings and heels
Fishnets, no reels
I'm starting to sweat, addictive as meth
Hold up! I just lost my breath

Clock, clock, clock, clock
My heart dropped
Because you're still so hot
U know I do not drink, but I think I'ma need a shot

So, woman, when you're buying
Think of sexy and defying
If you're walking, I'm trying
To see how those calves are complying

Think of me, yes, I want to see
What about the height
What about the sight

Woman in heels, you ain't tall enough for me

Look at the split in that dress
As I've digressed
The heels have confessed
How you've been blessed
So what I'm a mess.

My grandfather taught me, how to climb a tree
So, woman continue to be, the woman I want to see
Cause I'm about to sit down and make my plea
I'm not going anywhere; the show begins at 3

VOLUME III

CHOCOLATE ROSE

Standing on my feet, It's now 3 o'clock
And I'm tired of this damn tick tock.

I can't wait to see, my chocolate rose
When I see her, my imagination will grow.

Counting the hours, longing 4 her
Rubbing her gently, my kitty bout' to purr.

The bud of the rose is made just like her hips,
The tip of the rose, just like her lips.

The petal of the rose resembles her skin
So soft to the touch, it must be a sin.

The color should be red, by mind is coco
She'll make me holla, till I say no mo'.

I am the antidote, she is the cure,
No matter the day, the reason is pure.

And if her day is worse than mine,
I'll pluck those thorns, Damn my time.

See, you are the reason, I want to come home
The one reason I dare not be alone.

No other flower can compare
For the one I have is OH! So rare.

Such a blossoming flower, I want to see pose
As if in a garden, you are my chocolate rose.

MR. WRONG ON YOUR ARM

I'm your Mr. Wrong, but you make me feel oh so right
Despite, you sometime get mad at my very sight
Right! I still see the love in your eyes when we fight
The passion of the fight, makes the love making ignite

You throw me up on the wall, because you're mad to no end
This seem to woo me, and also made me grin
Kissing me as if the end is near, I want to deny this my fear
Listen to these words loud and clear

Done a lot of dirt in my time,
always thought of you when the light shines
I run to you when I'm in a bind,
So damn hard for me to walk the line

I know you're not mine, why are you so kind

You know I'm no good, no romance in my walk
But I enjoy a simple talk, covering u from the cold hawk

Here's money for you, what did you do
You looked past my street jail, you looked for the who

I eat no real meal, I'm alone is how I feel
I know you ask what's the deal; U just can't be for real

Leave the streets alone, you're grown, come make me moan
Let's make this a home, stop being a dog fetching a bone
Baby I know I'm your Mr. Wrong, you are attracted to my traits that's where I belong
Yes I'm wrong, yes it's been long, the music once heard is now the wrong tone

Love or my gun, my 44 brought me a lot of fun
Let us ride with the sun, binded to a greater bond

Here my 44, washing out to sea, I love me

I'm Mr. Right baby, but wrong she knows is still in me.

LADY I KNEW

She said, You are my friend
I said, What a beautiful spectrum when two colors blend

She said, I don't want to be left again, you're my friend
I said, You're dealing with a man, whose back won't bend

She said, I feel your soul, invading my eyes
I said, I'm wiping the tears of the heart that cries

She said, Your hands are on these voluptuous hips
I said, My focus is to kiss, the soul of your ruby red lips

She said, I felt your soul and started to tremble
I said, allow me the love, and it will be that simple

She said, would you please tell me why?...
I said, Shh! Because my heart says try

I'm the real deal, with a bonafide will
Now search your heart, and divulge your zeal
My soul, your soul, we're eagles we fly
No elated meal, my heart will die

I laid my head, where life is born
I said, to the Lord sound that horn
I found my why, it's you, I adorn

THE PAINTING AT THE GALLERY

The gallery was empty, one painting significant
Some were ok, but this one was magnificent

Those Arabian eyes, with a particular stare
Like the horizon of the sun, no orbs compare

The skin was unequaled, fashioned by light strokes
A hue of a few colors, the shades evokes

He made the lips full, with a color so deep
Complementing the dress, nails and feet

The stance was tantalizing, audacious in nature
Like the colors within, Oh a blue ice glacier

My appetite is for, the thicker persuasion
As my eyes have, an orgasmic invasion

She's spicy like herbs, from the down south cajun.
Curves like the ocean, they're roaring and ragin

The artist so focus, with precise detail
Comparable to the moon when a riverboat sail

I was on a date, with a woman in a frame
Never knew her, never met her, but she was driving me insane

The leaves were rustling, as she stood in those heels
As if they were cheering, for this full coarse meal

This painting looks real, I need to seal the deal
Do I owe anything, What the hell! Damn the bill!

Her hips were insatiable, like bees would be to honey
I must have this on my wall, Attendant! Here's my money

As he handed me this picture, I was in a daze
I was so amazed, engaged, Yep I was fazed
By this work of art, that was on this page.

And then I felt hands, that grasp my wrists

With the smell of perfume, the aroma persists

Excuse me, why were you staring at me
I'm sorry, I thought you were an exhibit, at the art gallery

YOU GOT ME

The tighter she wraps those legs around me
The loser I become to thee
At that moment we became free
One became we

SHE TOOK ME

She arrived home
Not alone
Not to enter her place

Parking lot scene
About to convene
Hearts commenced to race

Her eyes did pierce
His grip fierce
Glossy lips to kiss

Tune is slow
Seductive flow
Taxing for them to resist

Her breast pressed
His head rests
Hand to hips, her instigating moan

Cleavage is offered
His shirt altered
Swaying to the beat of the song

The moon is the spectator
He's the curator
Steady he guides those hips

Evaporating time
Her tingling spine
seductively sucking those lips

She controls his lap
His seductive rap
While unable to smile

She holds his neck
Loses a sec
Both uncontrollably wild

Surprising night
Stunning sight
Hypnotic place to be

I'm so tired

Extremely wired
Thankful that it's me

REDEMPTION IS NOW MY FAME

I've been to my personal hell,
Trapped inside this spiritual cell,
Tortured by this demon called fell,
The demon didn't know I was born to rebel!

Now it's my turn to bring the pain,
Demon you about to feel your own flame,
Power running through my veins,
As I break another chain,
I can't remain the same,
But part of me is a shame,
While I laid there lame,
Crying about the pain,
Redemption is now my fame,
I'm about to make it rain pain,
To the Falling Demon that brought the same!

This is my place,
Lord, bless me with amazing grace,
About to do battle face to face,
It's not a race, without a trace
Its do or die, world you better brace,
Demon you about to get a taste
Of a born warrior, his hits thump with BASS!!!

Walking through a forest of trees bearing no joy limbs were "Po",
Until I came across, one tree with a miraculous glow!

This tree confronted my eyes, made me rises,
I dealt with my own lies,
Rebirth, the old me dies!

Damn, I got a crown, forget the frown,
It's all smiles, this is my ground,
I've been bound, down, clowned, not understanding I'm renowned!

This was my world from the beginning of birth,
I've been hurt treated like dirt,
I now revert, to insert, my worth,
beyond the EARTH!!!!!!!!!!!!!!!!!

FALLING DEMON, YOU JUST GOT HURT!

THOSE SEXY EYES OF YOURS

Those eyes are reared by the sea
From a land far from me
The shape of those eyes dated to a time of 3000 B.C.

Never in a day eyes worth so much
Never a physical touch
Seductive as Rio, or passion as such

Eyes so stern like Louisiana deep
No sign of weep
A jade stone, her material is not cheap

The connection she gives, could tame a beast
With her eyes she'll feast
Her desire of appeal won't cease

I've been around the world twice
And seen expensive things with no price
No eyes compare to her entice,
Like a desert man to a block of ice
I have many habits, but her eyes, are now my vice!

Captured by a spell and yes, I'm memorized
Basically paralyzed
Strangely enough I feel energized

I feel like an addict with no control
Her eyes got a hold
She captured a piece of this neglected soul

She seems to speak without a word
I still heard
As she walked the curves, intentionally they swerved

This man is about to take a stand
I'm a big fan
Of those sexy eyes, 100 grand

I've been around the world twice
And seen expensive things with no price
No eyes compare to her entice,

Like a desert man to a block of ice
I have many habits, but her eyes are now my vice!

UNDYING LOVE

I am the man that stands in time
Hoping one day that you'll be mine

Watching the time as I count the hours
Waiting for that day our love will shower

You are the one that tamed my fire
Who lit my soul and filled my desire

There is just so much one can say
Of the joy you bring to me everyday

I wish time would stand still on a dramatic scene
Romantically engulfed, like a drug fiend

You are my joy, you are my heart
You are the root, you're my black art

You are the star, You are the night

You are the person that revived my light

You are the one that I turn to hold
You are the one that captivates my soul

Are the words I say a little too much
Or are the word I convey have the right touch

I'm humbled to your love, as yours pours out
With each drop of sand, I learn what you're about

May these words be forged into your heart
And forever integrated and always apart

I FELL FOR YOU LADY

I fell in love with you
Not for the way you make me feel
Not for what you do for me

Are you the real deal, my fulfilling meal?
My pill, so I can heal
Your shield
Woman are you my zeal?

I fell in love with you
So deal, I seal
Because of what you do for me

What do you see, in me
Do you see what I'll be
Am I oak tree?
For you and me.

I'VE NEVER HAD

I've never had a mature woman do this to me
Made me free, so I could see

I've never had a mature woman capture my site
Like a moth attracted to burning light

I've never had a mature woman appear so fine
Body intact, could sway the mind

I've never had a mature woman look at me so deep
Like at dinner, and I'm the last bite to eat

I've never had a mature woman with grace in her walk
Each step on purpose, each step I gawk

I've never had a mature woman know how to call my name
Make you drive at night, in the midnight rain

I've never had a mature woman, that knew how to touch
She could make you shift gears, step on the clutch

I've never had a mature woman, so seductive
One flinch, I might be her abduction

I've never had a mature woman, with that fashion
She's the drug, I'm crashin'. Dressed for passion

I've never had a mature woman that was so super
Do you tutor! I had never had a cougar

MY GIRL NEXT DOOR

It's you I adore,
To the core.
You don't bore,
Passion you pour.
I walk through the door,
You're heroin, I need more.
So watch me soar,
From the love I adore.
Forevermore,
Your love makes me roar.
As I explore,
I won't ignore.
My Peace and War
My romantic chore
I'm the ceiling, she's the floor
My girl next door

88 KEYS OF SEDUCTION

88 Keys of Seduction, as I was becoming an abduction
With multiple instructions, she was putting on a production

Learning to play the piano was a dream
I found an instructor so it would seem
But in her eyes was a seductive gleam

This lady came out in a dress of lace
Walking with elegance and grace
With a devilish grin on her face

Fragrance so tempting, as she sat near
Her hips so soft, my sweat began to appear
Play the G Key she whispered in my ear

She grabbed my finger and played the key
I was so nervous as a pupil could be
The note and her were seducing me

88 Keys of Seduction, as I was becoming an abduction
With multiple instructions, she was putting on a production

This piano lesson was getting me worked up
Her hand on my thigh was a setup
She never stopped playing a key, was her cover up

She's boxed me in, where I couldn't run
Might as well have so fun
Now the expression on her face, she's outdone

Your actions have been big and bold
Now I'm the one in control
I'm about to tempt every being of your soul

88 Keys of Seduction, as she was becoming an abduction
With multiple instructions, I was putting on a production

I picked her up, like a soul rising to the sky
Set her on the keys, My My My
No, I'm not shy, about to loosen this tie

I played the keys with a soft melody
My head in her bosom, she's now my celebrity
While her and this melody are played selfishly

My piano hands have already been skilled
The music sheet is the menu, surprise, you're the meal
As I play these keys, the vibrations you feel

88 Keys of Seduction, as she was becoming my abduction
With multiple instructions, I was putting on a production

It's 88 keys on the wood
She never knew I was this good
She thought I was from the neighborhood
Now the teacher has been matured

88 Keys of Seduction, as she blended with the percussion
From my introduction, music lady, we had a mutual induction

TO THE LETTER

The spies from my heart
Spoke of my love
Who I think the world of

She traveled by way of the wind
By fate becoming my friend
With her nothing can contend

It is said under the full moon
Things blossom soon
Our love can consume
Every atom in the room
Until we pop and boom

Intense words of passion
As you strut your fashion
Some flesh you ration

Love made like an arrow
Penetrating a yarrow
Our love never narrow

Let me kiss those cheeks
All 52 weeks
We're each other's freaks
Reaching our peaks

Making each other better
To the letter
Leaving each other never
As we survive the stormy weather!

LET ME GET THOSE BEANS

I'm so pissed, I don't want you in my sight
I barely know where you are half the night

Dexter, you treat me so wrong
An then come home singing that same ass song

I'm your woman, you're my man
Are you telling me, this is the last stand

I have asked for something simple, maybe just a flower
At least you could pick up the phone, during rush hour

I know you're mad
I know what it seems

If you gotta walk, before you go
Will you cook me a pot of yo beans

I may be overweight or not the right size
You never make me feel like I'm the winning prize
I uplift your spirits, I uplift your mind
I cook your dinner, so you will have a place to dine

Just for a moment, you don't have time
Not even for my piece of mind!

I tend to you needs; I gave you a seed
Remember, I patched your ass up, when you would bleed

I know you're mad
I know what it seems
If you gotta walk, before you go
Will you cook me a pot of yo beans

I work to keep a roof
Here's my paycheck, that's the proof

No rush hour call, my mom has been sick
So no, I'm not being a prick

You've picked up some pounds, those hips are wide
When I pull you near, I let these hands glide

I know you're mad
I know what it seems
If you gotta walk, before you go
Will you cook me a pot of yo beans

So baby understand, I need you around
I'm just trying to get us, on solid ground

I ask once again, to my lady
The one woman who had my baby

The beans the first night, we became friends
The beans that began our life, as we transcend

I know you're mad
I know what it seems
If you gotta walk, before you go
Will you cook me a pot of yo beans

You could wash dishes so I could cook Dexter!

THAT DRESS THAT NIGHT

Can I get you back, in that dress
The one that shows, you've been blessed

The one that makes, me a shaky mess
That dress, that no other woman can contest

That dress that has my eyes going, east to west
The perfect fit for your breast

Makes my heart forget about rest
Funny thing is, I don't see much flesh

Damn she's trying to make me guess
But I promise that dress makes me say yes!

So many, just plenty, curves to digest
Entice, excite, would you please check my chest

Under pressure, concern and even stressed
Look lady, this clothing I must address

I never thought I would be on a quest
For a dress, that's been put to the test

I'm about to invest
With this caress
So don't protest

Driving me insane
Until I can't contain

I'm going into cardiac arrest
About her and this damn dress!

*IMPOSSIBLE IS WHAT IT IS
UNTIL UNSTOPPABLE HAS THE AUDACITY TO CHALLENGE
IMPOSSIBLE.*

—ADRIAN D. WEAVER

*STARTING OUT AVERGE IS NOT A CHOICE
BUT FINISHING UP AVERAGE IS A CHOICE*

—ADRIAN D. WEAVER

Everyone wants a miracle

but no one wants to through the pain to get the miracle

—ADRIAN D. WEAVER

Made in the USA
Monee, IL
03 April 2021